WHERE DO WE GO FROM HERE?

Scientific evidence proving the existence
of the soul after physical death

PETER J HUDSON

Editor and Associate Barbara Bush

MAYFAIR PUBLISHING

Copyright Peter John Hudson 1999
First Edition 1999

Published by Mayfair Publishing
PO Box 860, Eastbourne
East Sussex BN20 7DJ
United Kingdom

ISBN 1 898572 03 8

Book design by Michael C Bush

No part of this book, except for the named quotations, may be
reproduced in any form without permission in writing from the copyright
owner, except by a reviewer who is welcome to quote brief passages.

This book is dedicated to the memory of Linda McCartney, a very beautiful, highly evolved spiritual being, whose purpose in this life was to give unselfish and compassionate service for the good of all.

Her golden light and unconditional love remains with us. It is to be hoped that they will stir within many the desire to follow the very same high examples in helping and loving all of God's creation, thereby, in the process, assisting them to evolve to a higher level of consciousness.

May her pure love and light continue to illuminate Planet Earth.

Peter Hudson
January 1999

Contents

First words 1
Introduction 2
Just across the stream 5
The sun of the south 7
Where do we go from here? 8
Remembrance 36
Science and healing 37
All God's creatures 42
Vegetarianism and spiritual practice 47
A meditation for loving kindness 54
Learning through lifetimes 57
Heredity 60
Jouissance 61
Builder of hedgerows 62
Words of wisdom, comfort and beauty 64
Celtic Blessing 84
The Author 85

Index 87

First words

Quantum physics is at last accepting that our entire Universe, including each and every one of us and all forms of life, is in actual fact, vibrational energy, light and sound. All life as we perceive it is eternal.

The author sincerely hopes that those who have become confused and lost, or unsure of what happens beyond the veil of death, and all those who have suffered, or are at present experiencing the trauma of bereavement, will find comfort, hope and the answer to man's most important question *"Where do we go from here?"*.

Peter Hudson

Introduction

Where do we go from here? A simple enough question but is there anyone truly qualified to answer?

Whilst we wear this dense physical body, this life support system that is so necessary for the spirit vibration to experience the lessons of Planet Earth, there are very few who can focus their minds sufficiently to penetrate the distance between this world and the next. It takes years of dedicated searching and commitment to the world of light.

Peter Hudson has had this commitment from his earliest years. Forty years and more of learning, practising and teaching in the field of holistic and complementary therapies, have taken him a little closer than the majority of us to the unknown world where we will all return when our earthly lessons are learned.

Peter has supported many patients through the last months and days of their illnesses. Being a natural health practitioner he doesn't get to see them when they are well. Only when the body or mind begin to fail in some way do they turn to him for help. There are times when he is unable to reverse the process of disease and ageing and can only offer support and spiritual guidance, both to the patient and their family. He sees death and its approaches more often than most.

Why do we leave it so long before we seek the truth of our ultimate destination? Day trips to the seaside or a fortnight's holiday in the sun are planned down to the finest detail. Let us at least show a little interest in the greatest journey we will ever undertake. If we seek the truth and the knowledge it will be given to us. Those who have gone before are offering their hands to us. Let us not be afraid to take those hands and allow them to show us the way forward.

Most of us have already lost someone dear to us. Many have yet to face that loss. Do we not want to know where they have gone once the life force has left the physical body? Will we know them again? How? Where? When?

Let Peter give you the benefit of his years of searching for the truth that lies beyond the final breath. He has researched many scientific reports and investigations, revealing the form of the life force and its ultimate destination. He has made his way through the mountains of paper so that you may find his conclusions in simplified form. Read them, question them, then start to seek the truth for yourself. One day you will find it. Be prepared and ready to begin the journey home.

Absorb the words of Silver Birch, the Red Indian guide of Maurice Barbanell, and know that you are in good hands:

> *"If you can help just one soul to find itself, if you comfort only one mourner, if you heal only one sick person, then the whole of your earthly life has been justified. How privileged you are to be aware of the tremendous power that is around and about you, that enfolds you, guards you, directs you and ensures that you will continue to unfold your latent divinity and the gifts which are your cherished possession."*

Know that this book has been written, compiled, edited and designed with love. Now it is to be read with love for all humanity and all God's creatures, past, present and those yet unborn.

In the words of Mother Theresa:

"I am God's pencil; a tiny bit of pencil with which He writes what He likes. God writes through us and, however imperfect instruments we may be, He writes perfectly."

Barbara Bush

I was never destined to meet Linda as we walked through this earthly life, but through Peter Hudson I knew her and loved her. I shared the last months of her life on some other plane, higher than this, intangible and unknown. When she reached the end of her journey my thoughts went to Peter and Linda's family.

I was aware of her last moments; they were shared with us. And from the picture in my mind of a truly loving family, the words of *Just across the Stream* were born. It was never intended for public view, only as a consolation for those most dear to Linda, but somehow she encouraged me to release these words to the world. They have been used in an altered form within my own family but this version, the original, is Linda's. Use it as you will, both for understanding and for comfort at times of loss.

May she continue to work with us from the higher viewpoint. Let her mind touch ours through the flimsy veil that separates us. We know so little of the world that awaits us and which we once called home.

Linda; when you are ready, we are waiting; we are listening.

Just across the stream

The great stallion lengthens his stride as we reach the open meadow. We have travelled far this delightful morning. The English lanes are bright with Queen Anne's Lace; the hedges sparkle with the pure white stars of blackthorn; the new spring grass is crushed beneath the hooves of the powerful horse. I feel the warmth of the rising sun on my face, fresh breezes gentle on my skin. Birds sing high above me as the beech trees break into new life. This is the perfect day.

I am not alone on this beautiful morning. I ride in company with those most dear to me, with whom I have travelled this earthly road. Together we have shared the lessons of this lovely planet; learning, teaching, accepting, growing. Individuals, we are held close by bonds of unbreakable love.

We share a moment of close communion, mind reaching out to mind; loving heart touching loving heart; soul resting against soul. There is no need for words. The heart says it all.

Reaching the edges of the open meadow, I draw a little ahead of my companions, entering the solitude of woodland. On all sides, swathes of vibrant bluebells greet me, their delicate bells pealing and chiming with a music that only I can hear. Their fragrance, delightful in its purity, welcomes and envelopes me. Petals the colour of celestial skies are soothing to the soul.

I dismount from the horse, leaving him grazing in a sunny glade. We will meet again, my faithful companion and I. I stroke his soft nose and thank him for the miles we have travelled together. A moment of mutual fellowship and I walk into the freshness of the bluebells.

Shafts of pure light break through the branches of the giant beeches. I look up into the canopy of the trees, following the light with earthly eyes. The brilliance permeates me. I know I must become one with this exquisite radiance.

Following the light but enfolded within the love of my companions, I reach the stream of flowing water. One last look at those I hold most dear, one last thought, and I cross the crystal waters, stepping stones at my feet guiding me towards the far bank.

Loving hands reach out to help me climb the steep slope. I am guided and supported; greeted by familiar faces; wrapped in the deepest, purest love.

On the far bank my earthly companions wait. They cannot yet follow me across the stream but they too are enfolded within this cloak of love. I can see the thoughts of their hearts; the deepness of their emotions. I can see, hear and feel more clearly than before. I have entered a new, unknown world. I will be waiting here when it is their turn to cross the stream. I cannot take away from them the new lessons they must learn.

Guided by loving hands and familiar faces I am led towards a grassy bank. Here I rest in the warm radiance of eternal light. I will heal. I will sleep. I will dream. Ahead of me lies a new life. I will not forget the old on the planet of learning but there is so much that I can do from here. To the sound of tinkling bells I become the light; the light that permeates all things.

I am home. I am where I truly belong
For Linda, with Love

Barbara Bush

The sun of the south

The sun of the south,
The stillness of mountains.
Both are still;
Essence and blood for eternal life!

The life behind personality;
The life of eternally wandering souls.

Who are we?
From where do we come?
To where do we go?

How magnificent is the essence of the earth;
How tiny compared with the eternal
kingdom of our Father.

From Taoism

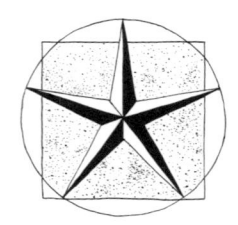

Where do we go from here?

A report on scientific investigations, personal experiences and observations proving the survival of the human personality beyond physical death.

The greatest physicists of our time, Einstein and Planck, recognised that an energy exists beyond the material world; a creative power that brings about the marvellous law and order of the Universe and of each being and object within.

Most of the world's religions describe the Creator of the Universe, God, as Light. God could also be compared to electro-magnetic energy; a source which manifests as light.

It is agreed that God is Love and we read in the Holy Bible that God created man in his own image. Therefore God's love manifests through all creation, not just within ourselves, humankind, but throughout the whole of the animal kingdom; nature; everywhere.

God is Energy; an energy which is not tangible but which many people feel within them and around them. Albert Einstein reminds us that energy cannot be destroyed. It can only be converted from one state to another. Energy and matter are the same universal substance, simply vibrating at different frequencies.

Recent advancements in quantum physics suggest that the Universe is made up of 98% energy and only 2% matter, so it is a great puzzle that we seem to focus far too much, and place too much emphasis, on the physical and material aspects of our being instead of the energy that created it.

Returning to Albert Einstein and his favourite equation, $E = MC^2$ which means simply that energy (E) may be converted to mass (M) and mass (M) may be converted to energy (E). When mass or matter is crushed it results in the release of considerable energy. This energy can be calculated as sub-atomic particles which correspond to the speed of light.

For us to find all the answers to the meaning of life as we know it, here in the Universe, we must first of all need to reconcile our physical being with the spiritual. All around us we see in the physical world continual destruction and regeneration. However, we see in the spiritual world either a permanent resting place for the soul or a further reincarnation on earth, the possibilities of which can be governed by our free will or choice.

Any thinking person really has to question why this state of affairs exists at all. Why a physical body and why the spiritual body and why would a creative intelligence destroy that which has been created? Therefore, in order to answer these questions, we must return to the very nature, the very core of our being and the creative energy, God; force. Jesus Christ said "I and my Father are one". God is therefore electro-magnetic energy and the very essence of Love.

All of us are a universe within a universe. I am you and you are me and the simple fact is all we have to do is love our Creator, God. It is my feeling and conviction that our soul, our personality, our identity, cannot and will never cease to exist. Neither will the spirit of any of our loved ones who have departed from this earthly dimension. They will never die.

Death, in my opinion, is certainly not the end as birth was not even the beginning, for our spirits existed before birth, and will continue to exist beyond death to function in an assigned, and deserved, spiritual dimension. Death as we know it is only an incident and a law of life.

William D Morgan said: "There is little in this life that proves to be permanent, therefore this makes it hard to comprehend eternity". Further, it is said, whatever principles of intelligence and learning we attain to in this life, it will be taken over with us into the next. Should a person gain more knowledge and intelligence in this life through his or her diligent practice in spiritual laws, they will have so much more of an advantage over others, especially when they make the transition into the spiritual realms.

I have investigated all manner of scientific findings and research, and seen reports on the continuity of life beyond the physical for well over forty years. With dedicated study and experience, I am convinced beyond all shadow of doubt that every one of us, including all the creatures, survives the physical death of their earthly bodies.

From my own field of observation, I have had, from an early age, several experiences of leaving and being outside of my physical body. I can remember well at around the age of 12 and my early teens, on numerous occasions on retiring to bed, and for no special reasons, I suddenly was aware of some part of me expanding in all directions from my physical body. I found myself floating or gliding in a horizontal position some several feet above and some two feet or so to the side of the bed. The sensation was not frightening or threatening. In fact, when I became used to it, it was most agreeable.

Incredibly, I was able to move forwards and backwards by moving my arms, just as if I were swimming on my back. I was even able to go forward as if I could go right through the window and out of the house. On one occasion, during the summer months, I could see people moving about and working in their gardens and I could see the roofs of houses and other familiar landmarks that I knew.

I have also had experiences when I have been walking, more often than not in peaceful surroundings over the countryside, of being detached from my physical body as if I were looking down on my physical self.

I have even had experiences that I was detached from my physical body when running. For many years I entered marathons and long distance running events and daily trained by running over long distances. On several occasions I experienced most pleasant and enlightening spiritual experiences of being out of my body; being at one with nature up amongst the treetops in the blue sky.

These experiences have been proof to me that the spiritual body is separate from the physical body and that my mind is in full awareness and, in actual fact, appears to have a greater capacity when out of the physical body, to understand the very origins, the laws of our being and the Universe. I have also experienced in meditation a similar course of events, and have felt myself rising outwards as if through my head, being conscious of the Universe beyond this physical plane.

I would consider myself, not a medium, but a sensitive, a mystic and also a visionary, for I often get impressions and feelings of various events, not just in a limited way, but world-wide before they actually occur here on the physical level.

I am now going to explain to you some scientific breakthroughs which prove irrefutably that we all survive after the death of our physical bodies. Much of this evidence, this scientific evidence, has been ignored by the orthodox establishment.

We all have our physical body which is made up of protons, neutrons and electrons. However, we also have an invisible energy body that consists of much finer, or subtle, sub-atomic particles that are contained within the same atoms as our physical particles. At the death of our physical body, our mind carries on exactly as it did before but within the normally invisible energy body. Therefore, we carry on living in a very substantial Universe that for most people is out of range of our physical senses.

We must understand that reality also is out there and lies in the intangible or invisible aspects of the Universe.

It is now recognised by many physicists as a fundamental fact of nature, that an atom is a miniature solar system. What appears to be reality all around us is most deceptive, for the deeper reality belongs to the underlying physics.

Some physicists speculate that if it were possible to fall into a black hole we would find ourselves in another dimension or Universe. Now this is what happens at the moment of transition or death of our physical bodies. We wake up in another Universe.

90% of the Universe consists of an intangible, invisible mass. We look through a telescope at our galaxy, the Milky Way, or a far distant galaxy, and what we see is only one tenth of the mass. Therefore nine tenths must be beyond our physical senses, or must be something between the earth and the sun that is many million, million times more dense than water. If this were not so, there would be nothing at all to prevent our planet from colliding into the sun.

The proof of continuity beyond physical death will, I believe, come from within the atom. Our Universe, in a physical sense, is objective. It exists only through the intangible, unseen Universe which is subjective. We are earthly bodies, temporarily housed; not physical people as such, for our real bodies are light energy bodies.

The easy way to explain to lay people is that we have two physical bodies; one that is visible and finite that is made up of protons, neutrons and electrons. The other body is invisible because it consists of very much finer and faster vibrating sub-atomic particles.

I hope that my readers will quickly realise that our very brief stay here on earth is but for one reason or purpose only and that is to learn certain lessons which I call the classroom. We are all in the classroom of the soul; hence the biblical saying "As we sow so shall we reap".

Our environment in the real world, the spiritual world, on transition from Planet Earth, which is the school or university for the soul, is determined by the spiritual lessons and progress we have made whilst here, clothed in a physical body. In other words, we all graduate to the spiritual dimension, or level, that we have earned by the development of our souls.

At the Scientific and Medical Networks Seminar way back in the late 1970's, held in a packed hall at the Royal Society of Medicine in London and attended by over 200 professional people, many belonging to orthodox science, medicine and religion, Dr Leggett said "The wind of change is here." He asked "What is life's purpose and is death the end?" He went on to state that there is a more than high degree of probability that man can function independently of his physical body and that consciousness survives death. Dr Leggett then concluded that:

1. Man is no more than five or ten pounds of chemicals.
2. Man can function independently of his physical body.
3. Man's consciousness survives death.
4. In the death state, man undergoes some kind of judgement.

He added three further probabilities:

5. Man evolves in a series of lives.
6. Divine love, justice and perfection exist at the heart of the cosmos.
7. The purpose of the school of life is to educate pupils, with grace and skill, in whatever parts they are called upon to play and to become masters of the art and science of living.

The discovery by physicists, I believe, of sub-atomic particles is the greatest breakthrough in our history. It will give thousands, if not millions of people here on earth, the irrefutable proof that there is no such thing as physical death, only a change into a higher realm of consciousness. The entire Universe, the sun, the air we breathe, right down to our physical bodies and those of the creatures, consists of sub-atomic particles. They make up everything; proton, neutron and electron, for sub-atomic particles are the building blocks of our entire physical universe.

Now I wish to explain that, after we die, we continue to exist as individual personalities. What you are about to read has been proven by many dedicated scientists working in this field. We all know that our physical bodies break down and ultimately decompose after death. Now we have to look into the question as to is there some part of us which possibly survives beyond the physical, and if so, what is it?

However solid our physical bodies may appear, they are composed of highly complicated and unstable molecules which are constantly breaking down and being rebuilt with fresh agents derived from our food. Scientists can show, and demonstrate, that all the protein of which the body is composed is being continually renewed, and that there is a complete renewal of our solid parts every six months.

To realise how unstable the molecules of our bodies are we have to consider dead flesh. If we were to leave a piece of meat in the open for even a short period of time we would be more than aware that the unstable molecules were breaking down and decomposing.

So we have to look into the question as to what gives us life and keeps us going. In other words, what element or force prevents the unstable molecular structure of the human body from disintegrating, or falling apart? The very simple answer to that question is what we call life, or as many refer to it as life force. The difference between a living body, which is constantly breaking down and rebuilding itself, and a body that is dead is that mysterious factor, life force.

However, I feel that it is not really mysterious and, due to scientific tests, many workers in this field have made one of the most important discoveries of our time. That is, all life as we see it, and know it, from the human body down to the animals, and even the very lower forms of life, is controlled and shaped by electro-dynamic fields; life force, in other words.

A great jump in understanding the life force was made by Dr Saxton Burr, who was professor of neuro-anatomy at a major university of medicine in the USA. A colleague of Dr Burr was a Dr F Northrop who was a most distinguished physiologist and philosopher. In many scientific studies, and experience over very many years, Dr Burr and Dr Northrop and their colleagues demonstrated beyond any shadow of doubt that life force, or life fields as they termed it, controls development, growth and ultimate repair of all living beings from ourselves to the creatures, from trees right down to the smallest of plants.

Whilst the physical material of our bodies is constantly being broken down, and consequently being rebuilt, the life fields keep them together, or in shape. That is why we can still recognise a relative, or a long distant friend, after many years, even though all the material of their face has been changed by this constant breaking down and rebuilding of molecular elements, for it is the life field that shapes, moulds and forms the entire material molecules of our bodies.

Modern science has shown that there is a life field around the body. Way back in 1911, W Kilner stated that the body has three layers; the first 0.635 centimetres from the body; the second layer is about 5.08 centimetres from the body and the last layer is about 15.24 centimetres from the body and very faint.

Further research has shown that a type of electro-magnetic energy runs up and down the spine, thus creating a basket-like field around the body. This field contains electro-magnetic waves but is not electricity. It consists of sub-atomic particles. To put it in another way, the life fields are like an electronic corset in which we live and without which we would disintegrate.

Just before the death of the physical body, the life field disappears. Therefore the body cannot live without its life field and death and decomposition follow rapidly.

We can see all around us the building up and maintenance of all living organisms. Nature herself uses life force fields in order to build and maintain life as we know and see it. Bodies, not just human, also animal and the biological matter of plants, trees and grasses, all depend on an invisible life force; a life force that is quite intangible to us. Without that life force there cannot be, as we know it, life here on earth. Our solid physiological matter without a life field would quite simply break down into various elements, including the molecular structures which are the building blocks for the maintenance and control of human and animal life fields.

A good example of demonstrating the elements of which we are constructed is that the body of both human and animal very quickly reduces to but a few handfuls of ashes on being cremated.

A very big question in many people's minds is where do these life force fields originate? When they leave the body at death, where do they go and how do they exist? A very simple explanation is that these fields both originate and exist in the great space around and within the universe, without themselves being reliant upon matter.

It is also of considerable interest that Russian research, with various items of very sensitive electronic equipment, has actually proved that at the moment of physical death, a life force leaves the physical vehicle or body and can be traced by extremely sensitive equipment. An interesting fact has emerged from this research. It appears that this force hovers around the dead physical vehicle for some days, until the body is either buried or cremated. Long after these events, the individual force field can be traced somewhere in the space of the universe.

The Russians are most advanced in the study of sub-atomic phenomena. Their scientists, working in these fields, refer to our spiritual bodies as the bio-plasmic body. If we understand the Greek meaning of *bio* it refers to living beings and *plasmic* translates as malleable. The bio-plasmic body, or the spiritual body, is the actual covering for the mind and spirit that is made up from sub-atomic particles. It can be likened to a butterfly emerging from the chrysalis; in other words our old, maybe diseased, physical body.

If we look into physics it reveals that the subject matter is outside of our normal physical senses. It is interesting to comprehend that the actual vibrational speeds within our physical atoms are moving at a rate of up to approximately 670,000,000 vibrations per hour. This is the speed of light. The atomic vibrations of the unseen Universe and those that dwell in the spiritual realms are more than possibly moving far in excess of this.

I would like to quote a famous Zen Buddhist, The Mighty Giant.

"People have forgotten the immense power they carry within them. They have been hypnotised by common sense, by what people would think of them and by the words of man-produced authority. They believe that they are nothing more than physical body which could collapse at any time.

The real truth is, however, that you are a child of Buddha and as such you have infinite power.

When you have found liberation through meditation, you will realise your real stature as a giant of the Universe who looks down on this physical world. This three dimensional galaxy is but a mere puddle to the higher dimensions. The realms of human enlightenment, below the very highest of realms, appear so tiny that you must bend down to see them."

This Planet Earth is but one very small dwelling place in an infinite universe of dwelling. We are all governed by divine laws which enlightened individuals know are immutable. To pay no attention to these laws will ultimately lead to misery and suffering. On the other hand, working in harmony with them gives one inner peace, contentment, happiness and self-realisation which no material or selfish acts can ever do.

Our physical bodies and, in fact, all matter consists of interacting electro-magnetic fields which are vibrating at enormously high frequencies. For instance, the nucleus of an atom will vibrate at about 10 - 22 Hz. These are almost inconceivably fast rates. If we could take a look through high magnification at our solid bodies, we would find the so called solid reality lost to a rapidly vibrating matrix of energy fields. In other words, there is a vast vacuum of emptiness within our bodies but within the void, the emptiness, is a considerable, very subtle, form of energy which radiates within and around all molecular or cellular matter.

The energy that our bodies are composed of, the life force fields, are electro-magnetic and electro-static fields which go to moulding and shaping the make up of our bodies. These fields are strong. Their function is to hold the atoms and molecules together. As these fields move outside and around our bodies they obviously become weaker. I quote Dr Belot and Dr Allendy:

> *"When we consider organic life in the light of biophysics, we find that electric phenomena are at the root of all cellular life and we conclude that the end of everything is an electric charge."*
>
> *Dr J Belot*

"In the past, medicine and biology saw life as a simple chemical reaction, a completely mechanical exchange of atoms and molecules. We can therefore interpret it as exchanges dependent on an electric force so that the very essence of this phenomenon is moved from the atom to the electron."

Dr Rene Allendy

However, we are surrounded and permeated by many fields, the first being the iso-electric static field from the planet; secondly, the electro-static fields created within ourselves and by our own bodies. We have the magnetic field of the Earth, the electro-magnetic field, which can be very slowly vibrating waves influenced by changes in the atmosphere by the visible light spectrum and into the higher light spectrums which have a very high frequency radiation.

Then we must consider the gravitational field of the Earth, the planets, the Sun and the Moon.

We also have electro-magnetic fields which we ourselves have created. These fields are radio and television waves, portable phones, microwaves and very many others.

Our bodies are made up of numerous kinds of tissue. Certain tissues appear to interact with a particular type of vibrational energy more than others. Many vibrations, such as ultra-violet rays, radiate rays which penetrate our surface tissues. However, sound waves have the power to penetrate and reflect from tissues deep within the body and of course we are all affected, whether we are aware of it or not, by gravitational and magnetic effects.

Every form of life oscillates between sub-nuclear to atomic, to molecular to sub-nuclear. Therefore the reality is that we are in actual fact bodies in a state of vibrational energies, both light energies and sound energies. I would like to put it in another way. Our bodies mirror the entire Universe, right down to the working of each and every cell. We are pulsating beings within a vibrating Universe which is constantly in motion between the finite physical planes and the infinite universal realms.

The Universe, as I see it, is cosmic consciousness in a process of continuing evolution. We must understand that our brains are purely amplifiers of thought, not the source of the thought which is mind, universal mind. We, I feel, are really observers within physical matter. If we observe, look around, it is almost as if we are witnessing a film where all of humankind is going through an enormous act.

There are various meditation techniques which have been practised for many thousands of years by eastern people, which have become very popular over the last twenty or thirty years in the west. These techniques are the means by which we heighten our levels of consciousness beyond the physical, thus becoming one with God, the creative force. It appears when we are in these higher states of consciousness that we know all.

These deeper states of meditation have proven to slow down the entire metabolic rate of the body so that the body requires less oxygen. This has the effect of resting major organs such as heart and lungs, and lowering blood pressure levels. The nervous system becomes most rested, thus allowing our minds, remembering they are part of the universal mind, to become united with the great cosmic mind, God. Many find, through diligent practice, that they will attain experience of inner horizons, which open up in no other way possible during the active state of our being.

It has been proven by scientific studies that many people who practice meditative techniques heal themselves of all manner of physical and psychological problems. As the body, the physical vehicle, becomes empty through meditation of all physical or earthly sensations, the mind unites with the whole of the Universe where certain facts, which we would not be able to obtain in the lower conscious state, are available to us.

Meditation allows us to become one with the source of all creative intelligence and pure consciousness. That is the very life force behind all that we are aware of on this earth, including ourselves. During meditation, the world of nature, as well as the world of thought, is experienced through universal mind. Through meditation, it is almost as if we were tapping into a great pool of pure consciousness. However, in order to experience levels of higher, leading to pure consciousness, one must experience these forces personally. That can only be achieved through meditation which need not be complicated, or confusing, nor even involve the learning of difficult words or mantras. There are many books written on all aspects and techniques of meditation, but by far the best way of learning is to find a teacher of high regard, in order to be given the essential keys to successful practice.

One must remember that before the isolation of electro-magnetic waves, the concepts of both radio and television seemed mere fantasy. Now they are accepted and commonplace. It seems reasonable to assume that before very long, life force fields, mind force or mind energy, thought, will also become accepted and rooted in scientific circles.

We have to remember that it took a considerable period of time to convince people in the early days that the Earth was round. Long before the theory was formulated, it was thought that we could only have a purely objective idea or picture of this world and nature. We accepted that there were all manner of life forms moving here and there, unaffected by scientific vision.

Physicists today recognise that when they themselves make an observation, they actually disturb the system. Therefore the consciousness of the person observing must now be considered. We live in an invisible and ordered intelligent ocean of subtle energy, that penetrates and interpenetrates all our body cells and those of nature. I feel that we need to learn how to control this powerful unseen energy force, for if we don't intelligently and positively use it for good purposes, it can and will take the action of destroying that which it created.

I would like to explain briefly the yin and yang theory and chi energy or universal force. How it manifests itself through the two polar forces, yin, which is female, and yang, which is male. We must understand that good or bad health and the conditions within our lives are determined by the harmonious balance of yin and yang, north and south. An evenly balanced yin and yang means good health, but if the energy is displaced in any one direction it will create disease or illness.

It is true that by unification of Heaven and Earth, Heaven being yang and Earth yin, we become one with all creation. All life here on Earth requires energy in order to produce energy which we see as life; therefore matter and energy are closely dependent upon one another.

> *"The Taoists call positive energy Yang and attribute its origin to the sun and stars; the negative energy is called Yin and they attribute its origin to Earth. 'Yang energy' distinguished positive atmospheric electricity and, under the name 'Yin energy' the negative charge of the earth."*
>
> *Soulie de Morant*

> *"Chi manifests itself in this world as a sort of radiation that is invisible to the ordinary eye but can be clearly seen by advanced adepts who have cultivated this ability. Chi can also be detected and measured by sophisticated technology."*
>
> *Dr E Howell (50 years researching subtle energies)*

Many physicists state that matter is but pure, condensed energy, strength and power. Energy is the power that produces all dynamic phenomena, whether it be electricity, radio waves or even the nuclear bomb. It is energy that produces the end results.

If it were possible to liberate the energy from a handful of pebbles, the energy thus freed would be able to propel a heavy ship or tanker around this world hundreds of times.

It is interesting to realise that solar energy gives to trees and plants the power to produce and fix carbon dioxide in the air.

The human body consists of thousands of millions of cells. The cosmic universe also consists of thousands of millions of planets. Therefore we are a miniature universe within a very much larger universe.

I have said in previous pages that we have more than a body. We all know the physical body, but the mind we are unable to see or feel with our physical senses. This is due to sub-atomic particles that make up this second body moving at enormous speeds and therefore invisible to us.

A very famous professor, F Reines from California, stated, "the final outcome of research into sub-atomic particles will boggle the mind". Professor Reines worked with Dr Oppenheimer's team on developing the first atomic bomb.

God is electro-magnetic energy; the very epitome of pure unconditional love. Each one of us is a very small fragment of that God-created force or energy.

Provided we love unconditionally all of Creation, the overall measure of universal love must grow and expand.

We make this journey from God and are born here on earth. We go through various cleansing and purification processes and, on the way hopefully for most of us, we learn that we must do what is right for all concerned with pure love. Then the Universe will expand with more love.

We are the Universe. I am you and you are me. We must love

God, who is within every living being, unconditionally. That is the path to spiritual growth and salvation.

It does not profit, or hold one in a high position, by acquiring, here on earth, as much as possible from the material world. All that we own here - property, money, land, businesses - does not mean a single thing when we leave this planet. What is required however is knowledge and the capacity to help others; to do unto others as you would wish them to do unto you and, with pure and unconditional love, give it freely to all beings, including the creatures and nature. That way you are building spiritual funds in the cosmic money bank. Of course, we can't all live the life of a saint and go out into the world with nothing; however, we have to maintain a balance.

Materialism in all its various forms, especially today, and to which the masses through the mass media are so addicted, does not bring any lasting peace or happiness. It does not matter to God, our Father, what treasures you lay up here on Earth. Sooner or later, whatever you own, be it property, land, finances, expensive cars and all the other trappings of this over materialistic and selfish society, does not mean a thing. If you had the opportunity to jet around the world many times over, visiting all the great cities, or cruising around the world in great ocean liners, buying expensive clothes and other material goods, you would not find any true lasting peace or happiness.

It is possible to not even go out into the world in order to know it, for, through meditation and unconditional love of God our Creator, you have everything.

It is useless praying to God and asking for material things. We can pray to God for his help, in respect to the unfortunates and underprivileged, but just to have and be at peace, through meditation, is worth more than material rewards.

However, it is said that God moves in mysterious ways and the

God within you and me knows what you want. Very often the way will be shown in order for you to achieve this, but whatever your desires are, the end result must be for the good of all concerned.

In order for our soul's growth, we are here to learn and serve unselfishly and unconditionally. Service to others from the very goodness of your heart will be laying up spiritual treasures for your soul at a later date.

This Earth is only one tiny little speck in the whole of the Universe. It is possible that in future lifetimes we could transcend, having earned our place, onto much more highly evolved planets. However, should we, or our souls, not learn what they have come to this Earth for, we will obviously have to make many such journeys back here in order to learn what we haven't done previously. Therefore, it is futile spending all the hours of each and every day on material pursuits, including work, if, in the process, you lose yourselves to the reality as to why you are here.

I feel that the state in which we will find ourselves after we leave this earthly plane is determined by the level of spiritual awareness that we have attained during our physical life. Even that state, I believe, is but a preliminary stage. It is both consoling and inspiring to understand that through a succession of spiritual lives on other planets, our individual spiritual progress knows no limitations.

There is another scientific area in which we can prove that life continues beyond this very limited physical world. The statements of those who have died clinically and have been medically resuscitated have produced quite remarkable evidence.

There are many scientists who have investigated the near death experience. It is estimated that millions of people throughout the world have experienced life beyond the physical on clinical death, to the point where they were resuscitated. By the careful evaluation and examination of thousands of such experiences, scientific researchers have been able to identify many common elements involved. The greater majority of experiences suggest that, on leaving the physical body, the person experiences a complete freedom; total absence of physical restriction.

In case after case, people have said that they have been embraced by a bright and very pure light. In fact, the environment in which many have found themselves was nothing like any experience here on earth. The light is so comforting and loving that many resist returning to their bodies. Some have recalled being aware that they were in a beautiful garden filled with enormous flowers. The warmth, light, colour and sound were beyond human comprehension. Others have told of a great being of light surrounding them.

So many of these people who have experienced a near death situation have stated that it has completely changed their whole outlook on life as we know it here in the material world. Many businessmen have seen the futility of laying up, as it were, treasures on earth, and have given a lot of their time in helping the needy and suffering. For many it has completely wiped out the fear of death and, in some cases, many look forward to the time when they can return to those glorious light realms which they experienced whilst out of their bodies. Many report seeing relatives and loved ones, even animal friends.

The basic physiological material of which our bodies and brain cells are constructed, is ever changing, being constantly broken down and rebuilt. Dr Penfield's experiments on the mind, proving that the mind is separate from the brain, prove beyond all doubt whatsoever that mind and brain are completely different.

Dr Penfield also stated that the human brain is an organ that is conditioned. The brain can be likened to a computer. However, a computer has to be programmed. Therefore the brain itself also has to be programmed by the mind. I like to call the mind universal mind because we are all part of universal mind. So universal mind is the programmer of the brain, but is outside of the brain.

I think we can say definitely that mind, like life force or life field, is also a field; a field of its own and a more powerful field than a life force field. It cannot be electro-magnetic like a life field, and it certainly cannot be measured or detected. Physicists are now beginning to understand mind fields, or thought fields, and life force fields,

What they have concluded is that it is impossible to destroy either a life force field or a thought or mind field unless we understand its source. As that source is the creative intelligence behind all life as we know it here on Earth, the force is indestructible. Although matter is destructible, the force, both mind and life force, cannot be affected through destruction of the biological matter. When we consider mind, memory, thoughts, these forces are the very building blocks of our individual personalities which, again, cannot be destroyed. Therefore, there is irrefutable scientific evidence that the human personality is separate from the physical vehicle and, at the time of death, survives. In the process of doing so it transcends to a fitting place, or sphere, which it had earned whilst in the physical body.

So we can say that our real self, the energy body, the soul, the personality, belongs to the universal force, our Creator, and it is immortal; a mind. We must understand that the mind is not really the brain, as so many would assume. The mind is separate from the brain and the body, but, having said that, the mind controls energy, negative or positive. In other words the mind leads energy.

The mind is part of the great universal mind as the life field, or life force, is part of the whole universal cosmic force.

It is interesting to note that many scientists have noticed that changes in the actual life force, or field, can be detected. This can be demonstrated by sensitive electronic equipment and cameras.

These changes in the life field, or life force, can often be related to various physical illnesses.

For instance, the Russians have long known that changes in these fields, which can be measured, or seen, through Kirlian photography, can reveal indications long before disease actually manifests on the physical level. These subtle changes show up on the L field, or life fields or force fields, suggesting that various degenerative conditions such as cancer, cardio-vascular illness or neurological illness would stand a very good chance of not occurring on the physical level if we could treat at that time. When I say treat, I mean by the use of energy medicine such as homoeopathy, acupuncture, electromagnetic energy fields and meditation. Remember, mind leads energy.

Various forms of the self-healing arts such as Tai Chi Chi Kung and yoga, would then correct the subtle imbalances, restoring normality within the L field. This would prevent the likelihood of physiological destruction by a disease force.

We must realise that disease is actually a force, a negative force as opposed to a positive, normally balanced life force. It is energy, negative or positive, that influences the body for good or bad. More and more medical scientists here in the west are beginning to see this. There is in communist China, a medicineless hospital where people go with life threatening illnesses such as cancer, neurological disease and all manner of psycho-physiological problems. The medical attendants there, doctors trained in orthodox western medicine as well as traditional Chinese medicine, supervise through instructors these so called incurables without medication and special diets.

Through the very gentle self-healing art of Chi Kung they are taught to open their minds to lead the energy, the chi, the universal force, to the problem parts and to the body generally for healing purposes. It says a lot for the healing efficacy that they have more than a 70% success rate which has attracted many western medical scientists.

Here in the west, the practice of Tai Chi Chi Kung, in many cases and in great respect, is incomplete. Many of us think that all we have to do is to go through a few simple movements, very slowly, in as relaxed manner as possible, and that's it. But we must open our consciousness, our minds, up into the heavens beyond the blue sky; into the golden pure light realms of the universe; travelling the universe for that matter; seeing within the mind, the whole of the universe and all the various elements within. Then, with mind force, directing the energy, the creative force, the chi, into the physical body through various points, which we call acupoints, and energy centres.

I can testify personally to the efficacy of this medicineless system, for I have been practising Chi Kung and various forms of Tai Chi for very many years. Many of those whom I teach can also testify how highly effective these self- healing forms are, provided we allow the mind to direct the energy.

The physicist Fritjof Capra, in his book *'The Tao of Physics'*, states "in Chinese philosophy, the life field or life force idea is not only implicit in the notion of the Tao as being empty and formless and yet producing all forms, but it is also expressed explicitly in the concept of chi".

The father of the atomic bomb, Oppenheimer, the founder of quantum physics, Heisenberg, and Albert Einstein, have all compared principles of physics with eastern philosophy.

The gentle exercises of Chi Kung promote the weak electro-magnetic field of the body, therefore not only maintaining health, but also restoring it when it is lost. The mind then absorbs energy from the Universe, which can be transmitted to all forms of physical matter.

I shall now continue by giving scientific evidence in respect to the mind, and the power that the mind has on the physical. I will further explain why mind is separate, and even distinct, from the body and brain.

So, what is mind? It certainly must not be confused with our brains. The brain cells are constantly breaking down and being rebuilt by complex molecular functions. Therefore, in a brain that is being constantly broken down and rebuilt, if memory is part of the brain, memory of past events would quickly be lost in the breaking down process. However, memory, being an essential part of mind, can be demonstrated through medical tests to be permanent. Therefore anything which is permanent from physical mass must be completely different and unlike physical matter that is constantly changing.

Dr Penfield of the USA made medical history on many occasions by using a local anaesthetic to open the brains of people who were fully conscious. He discovered that when he used very delicate surgical equipment in order to stimulate certain parts of the brain with a low electrical impulse, it was revealed that very old, or elderly patients, could lucidly remember, and describe, all manner of experiences or events which had occurred when they were very young, even as children. They could relive those events during the experiment as if they were still in that time.

Dr Penfield discovered that stimulating the cortex of the brain with an electrode activated all past experiences. Many people underwent an unfolding of experiences and events as they occurred, in full detail.

A further interesting observation was that, during Dr Penfield's experiments, he found that stimulating the temporal lobe of a patient undergoing brain surgery actually created in that person a most lucid experience of leaving the physical body.

Many people have actually witnessed a light leaving a person who is going through the dying process. This light could be compared to an electro-magnetic force.

A Dr Deke stated, our brain is like a transmission with 500 gears and we only use a few of them.

Very often we come across cases where people who have had a near-death experience are spontaneously cured of a life-threatening illness. Researchers explain the reason for this as being that an out-of-body or near-death experience alters one's personal electro-magnetic force field.

I quote the famous professor of physics, Stephen Hawking, when he said: "God made all things. Not one thing in all creation was made without him. The Word was the source of life and this life brought light to humankind and all creation. The light shines in the darkness and the darkness has never been extinguished. The Word was in the world and though God made the world through Him, yet the world does not recognise Him."

I remember personally speaking to a patient who had had two out-of-body experiences during medical treatment. On each occasion she experienced, and still has, a most powerful memory of a truly beautiful heavenly scene, transfused with a kaleidoscope of colour, brilliant light and the most beautiful flowers that appeared to be singing and radiating a warmth and love which she could not compare to anything on the physical plane.

Every person's life can be broken down into five important steps. From birth, the incarnating soul has been learning to adjust to the new shape of the human form he has been born with. Up to the age of 7, the soul is preoccupied by the problem of how to gain attention to itself, and the co-ordination of bodily parts.

Between the ages of seven and fourteen he starts to develop emotions and a temperament. Everybody knows that fourteen is a point that is often referred to as the 'upheaval of adolescence'; the emotional body commencing to take over the physical body. From the age of fourteen this intensifies until the mind awakens at approximately twenty one.

From twenty one to twenty eight, the mind further develops until it begins to realise that there is more to life than was first thought.

From the age of twenty eight the mental body takes over and adjusts itself to the lower emotional and physical bodies. By the age of thirty five this should have completed itself. Therefore the person is, or should be, mentally balanced.

From thirty five to forty two there is an awareness of something else in life. This is due to the soul's desire which is endeavouring to control the mind.

From forty two to forty nine, this process increases further and during this time the person becomes aware of their actual soul.

From forty nine to fifty six, a realisation occurs that there is much more to life than selfishly over-indulging. Thoughts begin to enter the mind as to whether anything has actually been achieved of merit in their life, or was it all possibly due to vanity and the ego?

The conclusion is reached very often between the ages of fifty six and sixty three. The person either decides to continue his existence in the lifestyle to which he has been accustomed until it resolves itself or, very often, because of unrest of the soul or an imbalance between the physical, emotional and mental bodies, the person elevates himself to high spiritual levels through spiritual practices such as meditation.

The finite world in which we find ourselves is actually divided into the mineral, the vegetable, the animal and the human kingdoms. This finite world, along with and including all the other worlds and planets in this enormous galaxy, was originally constructed from tangible energy, or in other words, vibration. It has been said that

God, in the very beginning, was out there alone in a vast ocean of thought, and nothing at that stage of a tangible nature had been created.

All matter as we know it is simply vibration, including water. The oriental philosophers and Taoists postulate that everything is light energy. Jesus himself said that everything is light. This meaning of light simply refers to a rate of molecular vibration which, in its purest and highest forms, is impossible for us to perceive.

I would ask my readers, can you say that electricity doesn't exist, or X-rays don't exist simply because you can't perceive them? You can't smell electricity; you can't smell X-rays; yet they exist. Therefore, I feel that we have to eliminate from our minds that a thing cannot exist just because we cannot examine it with our five senses or with the naked eye.

If you hopefully continue to evolve spiritually, you will ultimately develop extraordinary sensory vision which will enable you to perceive the most sensitive wavebands of vibrational energy. If the human body had no senses and was inert like the mineral kingdom, it would be too inert to know that it actually existed.

Perhaps the earliest evidence in history that can be recorded on whether mankind has a soul can be seen in the works of Pythagoras around 540BC. He stated that he received the memory of all his previous lifetimes as a gift from the god, Mercury, together with the knowledge of what the soul experiences before birth and after death. Around 200BC Plato himself stated "Soul is older than body. Souls are continuously born again into this life."

I feel most strongly that we should see ourselves as developing spiritual beings within a collective universal evolution of consciousness. We must further accept and acknowledge all major religions and their various teachings. They may say in words that we are not familiar with that the only way to God is through obedience to spiritual and divine laws.

Let us consider that the great spiritual teachers throughout history, Abraham, Jesus Christ, Moses, Mohammed, Buddha and others, were all part of a divine plan in order to reveal to those who wished it a furthering of their spiritual knowledge and development; their purpose being to teach the truth through unconditional love.

Jesus says in the Bible that we must love our Father more than anything in this world and that our Father in the heavens is within us and every form of life. Therefore, in unconditional love for all creation, whatever shapes and forms it may so take, we must love the Father within.

In this day and age we are living in very uncertain and unsettled times. We only have to read what is going on worldwide and see on our television screens the various events that are unfolding throughout the whole of this Earth. Already we see signs that we could all be thrown, even in the western world, into a severe economic crisis, a recession similar to the 1920's recession where money will not be of any value at all. People's dreams and desires in respect to material gains will be lost.

We see social political unrest everywhere; a total disrespect for others; and we often wonder why there is so much suffering, so many conflicts. But if we really look at it at its deepest meaning, we see that we are to blame. Man's inhumanity to man will never cease until he becomes totally loving and compassionate to all creation, and that includes nature and the animals.

Throughout our daily lives, we should be regularly thanking our Creator for what we have; for the food that we have; for the comforts that we have. We should be living as far as we possibly can with natural and divine laws, not abusing our bodies in any way and that means less reliance on stimulants such as alcohol, nicotine, various prescribed and other drugs.

We can get all the help that we require from the natural kingdom. It is said that for every ill of man there is a simple and natural remedy. Most of us in the western world overeat. We see in the third world countries terrible famines, horrifying situations of malnutrition.

Here in the west we are suffering from a very different form of malnutrition; that is the consumption of empty carbohydrate and junk convenience type foods. We need very little to sustain our physical bodies, provided that food is natural and perfectly balanced. In fact, overeating robs our brains and our bodies of vital force and energy.

Under those conditions we cannot rise to any great degree spiritually. The wise man or woman eats and lives very frugally and, provided they follow divine natural laws, have found through meditation practices and periods of silence that they come to know God. They have inner security, inner peace and contentment which so many people who are following the material path and appear to be wallowing in the seas of wealth and materialistic goods, just don't have.

Remembrance

Death is nothing
I have only slipped away into the next room.
I am I and you are you,
Whatever we were to each other, that we are still.

Call me by my old familiar name,
Speak to me in the easy way you used.
Put no difference in your tone,
Wear no forced air of solemnity or sorrow.

What is death but a negligible accident?
Why should I be out of mind because I'm out of sight.
I'm waiting for you for an interval,
Somewhere very near, just around the corner;
All is well.

Canon Henry Scott
(1847-1918)

Science and healing

Atoms are no longer seen as the smallest indivisible part of matter; as the building bricks of which all material things are made and of which we are aware through our sensory experiences.

The atomic and sub-atomic physicists are now opening up a new marvellous and mysterious world; a world of ever-changing energy patterns; of waves and particles that are in constant movement, acting and reacting upon each other. These are amazingly affected by the mind of the observer so that the physicist can no longer remain detached from what he sees, but becomes part of the experience.

Matter can no longer be described as something solid that we can apprehend with our senses. The manifestations in the multitude of forms of this sub-atomic realm contain enormous forces and are governed by the new laws of physics, calling for new theories and concepts.

The atom is composed of particles of energy, electrons, which vibrate as they move around the nucleus in constantly changing orbits and bound to it by forces which keep it stable. The interaction between the electrons and the nuclei is the basis of all solids, liquids and gases and of all living biological processes associated with them. The diversity of the particles, their nature, properties, length of existence and the results of their interactions and collisions make a fascinating and most complex picture which is totally impossible to predict. The physicist reveals this to be not arbitrary and chaotic but a realm of movement, rhythm and even beauty wherein can be caught glimpses of the glory of God's creation.

As everything in the Universe is composed of atoms and is in effect the manifestation of this most marvellous sub-atomic activity, we have to seek a new scientific understanding of creation itself and ourselves, including all aspects of life, as part of it.

One of the most intriguing, mysterious phenomena which has been revealed by astronomers is the actual existence of Black Holes. In simple terms, this is an area in outer space in which matter seems to be disappearing. On the edge of the Black Hole it is suggested that we are once again on the verge of even newer laws of physics which we have not yet begun to comprehend. We are thus moving into new and uncharted waters, even deeper and subtler energies; impossible to conceive and with enormous creative forces.

The same pattern is emerging within ourselves as we begin to unravel the nature of the atoms of which we are composed. Fritjof Capra in his book *'The Tao of Physics'* states: "As we penetrate deeper and deeper into nature, we have to abandon more and more the images and concepts of ordinary language and on this journey to the world of the infinitely small, the most important step from a philosophical point of view is the step into the world of atoms".

Probing inside the atom and investigating its structure, science transcended the limits of our sensory imagination. From this point on, we could no longer rely with absolute certainty on logic and common sense. Thus atomic physicists provided the scientists with the first glimpses of the essential nature of things. Like the mystics, the scientists are now dealing with a non-sensory experience of reality and like the mystics they have to face the paradoxical aspects of this experience.

Although much is now known about the nuclear structure and

interaction between atomic and sub-atomic particles, we do not yet understand the nature of the forces within or the laws which operate at this level. Nevertheless, one can suppose that in this very complex world, the nucleus is not the ultimate, but within lie energies even more subtle and with even more creative powers.

The physicist is entering the realms of the paranormal, of the conscious and the sub-conscious mind and of the emotions; the source of the will, of revelation, inspiration and mystical experience. Deeper within is the power of prayer and love and the world of the Holy Spirit. In the macrocosm of the Universe and the microcosm within us, science is showing us the essential wholeness of all things. The concept that all things are of God and of God within. Surely, this the province of religion, indeed all religions. "I and my Father are one", as Jesus so often told his followers.

Within us lies the spiritual power which can bring harmony, health and wholeness. This is at the heart of Jesus Christ's healing ministry. It is no longer a purely spiritual concept but becomes also a scientific one. Even as the physicist must find even more patterns and laws to fit these theories so, it must be realised, are the laws quite different which govern the deeper levels of our being; laws which do not necessarily clash with those of science but are an extension of them.

I feel that the very first thing that we must endeavour to put into practice is to become aware of God's purpose in ourselves and, in fact, all creation and to align ourselves with it, that in us and through us His will may be done.

I would like to discuss bio-magnetism, the invisible force. All living creatures are made up of billions of cells. Each cell is an electrical unit behaving like a small battery. Each cell in the human body may be considered as an independent electrical unit. The cells vibrate and oscillate at distinct frequencies and receive their individual electrical bearing from the atmosphere. Thus we human beings, including the creatures, are mainly liquid in composition like a bag of salty water. Any fluctuating magnetic field in a conducting field sets up electric currents. We all depend on the beneficial influences of the Earth's natural rhythms. However, modern living has decreased the influential effects of the Earth's magnetic fields.

It was discovered many years ago that magnets could have a beneficial effect on health. Ancient cultures applied magnets to all sorts of injured limbs and used them in cases of ill health. Much research has been done in Japan and America in the use of staticmagnetics in healing a whole host of problems.

Never before have people been so absorbed in the pursuit of health and wellbeing. It is generally accepted that energy and matter are really one. Therefore the human body is as much energy, which actually consists of various wave-like particles, as it is solid mass. In view of this, I feel we should be treating physical problems as much with healing energies as with physical medicines. Treating the body as energy rather than mass is certainly not a new concept. It goes back to ancient cultures which are now beginning to gain acceptance here in the West, even by orthodox medical scientists.

I would like to explain a very simple and effective way of collecting universal healing energy or chi for the healing of oneself. This has originated from Chi Kung which is a very ancient self-healing art.

Sitting, standing or lying, put your hands close together so that the fingers and palms almost touch each other. Relaxing your shoulders and hands, slowly open your hands to the sides then close your hands until the palms and fingers almost touch. Repeat these opening and closing movements many times and soon you will experience some sensation between your hands; almost a sensation of electrical currents. These sensations are caused by the chi, the universal healing force gathering.

When doing the opening movement, imagine that your illness disappears into infinity, going beyond the blue into the golden light realms. During the closing movement, imagine that you are delivering golden light energy into where it is needed. Meanwhile, tell yourself with real mind intention that the universal loving chi is healing you and that you have recovered from your physical problem.

Repeat this exercise many times a day, slowly and with pure mind intent. The mind in actual fact leads the energy. Do not think of anything else except healing yourself with the chi and have a great respect for the chi energy. Know great love for all creation. During and after the exercise, give thanks to God for that universal healing force and for the great compassion and love.

All God's creatures

It is fitting within the ethos of this book to mention the spiritual evolution of the animal world.

All animals have a soul as indeed all living things have. By all living things I mean birds, trees, plants, rocks and soil. They have souls but a different type to man's. With their soul they have a place in the divine plan.

There are two main concepts concerning animal soul evolution. One believes that our soul experiences begin with the mineral kingdom, passing through the vegetable kingdom and from there to the animal stage which has more depth. The animal cycles begin with small insects and evolve through the animal kingdom with varying cycles of reincarnation.

So it is that we encounter every kind of living experience within the Universe from the mineral kingdom right through to the ultimate state of being.

Dogs are considered to be highly evolved, along with horses and elephants. This of course is an age old eastern theory, believing that the highly evolved animal souls form into a group and that group forms a new human soul. This has never been established and I cannot answer it, but it is thought that the oversoul who establishes the soul consciousness in the Universe does so on the premise that God resides in the image of his own likeness, that being a definite species, man.

The other concept is that animals evolve within a group of like souls. They are not required to pay for past mistakes with karma since they have no responsibility except that of love towards the human beings who love those animals. For instance, a dog who always puts master before self will evolve through that kind of thought and action but would ever remain canine to evolve eventually without a physical body.

Animals, I personally believe, especially our pets such as dogs, cats, horses, and rabbits, are able to find a higher form of consciousness. It is here that man's love towards these creatures helps them to form a spiritual sense as well as a human point. After the death of a well loved pet of whatever size, the love of the friend of the animal helps to keep the animal in the heavenly realms. They live for a time until the human friend passes over. They then both become reunited in the sea of spirit.

I feel very sad to think that so many people believe that because they are human beings, they are the only ones that have a spirit. When an animal becomes intelligent, it is through your love of this creature that this becomes possible. If that animal was just left to drift, it would have instinct but not thought. You can love an animal so much that it begins to think. You pass the current of your thought through that animal and its brain then starts to work in a much different manner.

As Jesus so often said: "In my Father's house there are many mansions." I believe that there are spiritual planes for our animal friends and also for the wild creatures that never receive the love of a human being.

Very many years ago, a good friend of mine gave me the following. The author is unknown.

'Our Heaven'

I have so often read or heard of people complaining that no idea is ever put forward definitely as to the kind of future life to which we can look forward, other than the old idea of harps and golden streets. They don't seem to have come across with any ideas of their own as to what they wish to do, and so I write this little article 'Our Heaven'.

I have always loved horses and dogs and I pray and believe that when I pass on I shall find myself in the Happylands, a Heaven made for them and to which they will be allowed to refuse entry except to those people who have loved and understood them. I hope to find in those Happylands a world where the word 'self' is unknown and its heavenliness is to love and to be loved by our beautiful companions and friends. The love is God. And I expect to find also that in their Heaven, all the animals will have evolved to a state where their intelligence is equal to ours and that we shall be able to converse together, probably by thought transference.

I like to believe that we shall have no power over them for we shall all be free people in our Heaven and that we shall be friends, trusting and loving each other.

If you should want a ride you will have to ask some equine friend to take you and there will be no saddles or bridles but just perfect trust between two friends, exploring together this wonderful heaven that God has given us. All around us our dogs will be ranging far and wide with an occasional bit of fun in the way of a chase provided by some kindly deer or rabbit, for we shall all be happy friends in the Happylands.

When Jesus Christ comes round to see how we are getting on, I don't want Him to find us down on our knees waiting for Him but working for His dear animals, cats, dogs and horses and of course the smaller brethren. And then will be the time to bow our heads in gratitude and to ask for His blessing on what we are doing; to ask that we humans and animals may be given power to heal and comfort those poor creatures coming over in pain of body or mind, probably largely caused by man's brutality, and to pray that we always have worthwhile work to do and the ability to do it.

In my imagination it's a very wonderful Heaven. How much more wonderful is the reality likely to be?

I would like to raise the issue of dominion over the creatures. The Hebrew word used in the Bible comes from the root *'radah'* and is extracted as *'yirdu'* and denotes a sense of stewardship or guardianship. In other words the Bible asks us to care for our more humbly endowed brothers and sisters; not to kill them and eat them. For instance, a king is said to have dominion over his subjects but that doesn't mean that he should eat them or abuse them. He must care for them, help them and even love them. This is the type of dominion the Bible is referring to.

I would also like to point out that the biblical verse that gives us dominion over animals appears in Genesis 1:26. Three verses later in Genesis 1:29 a vegetarian diet is recommended. In other words, God gives us dominion over the animals and only three verses later prohibits their use for food. Implicitly, the dominion he gives us cannot include using animals for food.

Also in Genesis 1:30, God makes it clear that animals do have souls. God says that all creatures, whether on land, in the seas or in the sky, have a living soul within their body. He uses the words *'nephesh'* for soul and *'chayah'* for living. These are the same two words used to describe the soul in human bodies. Therefore animals and humans have the same sort of soul, at least according to the Bible.

I believe that a true Christian must understand that he should fully consider the doctrine of extending Christ's love to all of God's creatures. If he does any less, in my opinion he is hardly a Christian. The Vedic saints and prophets on the other hand all endorse vegetarianism and kindness to animals. Many of the Christian saints were exceedingly loving and gentle to the creatures and surely we ought to show them great kindness and gentleness as well, above all because they are of the same origin as ourselves. St Francis of Assisi was a vegetarian as were many of the saints. It is interesting that the Gregorian saints, many years before Francis, were distinguished by their love for animals. They made friends with bears, wolves, deer and birds. As vegetarians they refrained from hunting.

The early Celtic saints too were in favour of compassion for animals and were also vegetarian. Wales, Cornwall, Brittany and Ireland in the fifth and sixth centuries after Christ went to great pains for their animal friends, healing them and praying for them as well. I feel that it is total hypocrisy if we pray for God's mercy and not show mercy to those weaker than ourselves. Violence begets violence. If we don't show mercy, why should we receive it? Rather, divine justice will be shown. As we sow, so shall we reap. This is called karma. Jesus referred especially to this.

Please remember that all the creatures are our brothers and sisters under God's fatherhood.

Vegetarianism and spiritual practice

Mankind's spiritual development has progressed from the dense vibration of the mineral kingdom, through bacteria and algae and varied forms of creeping things, to the more advanced world of animal life in its multitude of form.

In the world of spirit everything has its place. The development of the animals is interlinked with our own. When an animal dies, either from natural causes or with the assistance of man, its spirit will travel through the veil to the unknown world that awaits us all.

An animal that has been known and loved in its contact with man will develop a degree of soul consciousness which will help with its progression towards the ultimate. While a deceased animal holds the love and remembrance of those it has known on the earth plane, it retains the ability to communicate in the spirit world with those it has known and loved. We are part of the animal's progression; the animal is part of ours.

One of the hardest decisions we are ever called upon to make is when to terminate the life of a suffering animal, particularly in the case of a well-loved pet, the true confidante, companion, counsellor and friend. In the natural world the animal would be eliminated by predators or its inability to feed when age and disease take hold. But in the unnatural world of the pet or captive animal, their world is out of balance. Through medication, surgery, special diets and loving care, the animal's life span is prolonged instead of letting nature take its course. When the end comes, the animal's spirit will be aware of the intention and the love that goes to make the decision to terminate its life. Soul to soul, the animal's spirit has the capacity to know, understand and forgive the decision.

An animal bred for material use by man but without the love and consciousness of a relationship will return to a soul group consciousness. We find this group consciousness in our own world with the disasters that happen on a massive scale in famines, wars, floods and earthquakes. The souls of mankind and animals will return to spirit in their own particular similar groups.

It saddens me to know that very many lovely people who are treading a spiritual path eat the flesh of animals. I feel it is totally incompatible with true spiritual principles. Those who wish to aspire to a higher level of spiritual consciousness will, by choice, give up the eating of flesh.

The spiritual connections of a vegetarian or vegan diet are clear. *"Thou shalt not kill,"* I quote from Jesus Christ. If he had meant thou shalt not kill humankind, he would have specifically taught this. Yet he said *"Thou shalt not kill"*, which surely means all beings, whether they are human or animal.

Our animals are our friends and we do not kill our friends. Animals, like us, are evolving spiritually. To kill an animal is a violation against spiritual law which can only result in bad karma. God did not create animals for us to kill, to use in sport or for cruel experimentation. We are here to look after God's animal kingdom. We should be taking care of them. We don't wish to rule over them. If we take care of our family or our friends, we don't kill them and eat them.

If we can look an animal, bird, reptile or insect in the eye and make that spiritual link, how can we then take its life and eat it. It has looked at us with trust and unconditional love. Soul has touched soul; mind blended with mind.

By the unequal odds balanced against the animal world for the sake of sport we are violating spiritual laws and stopping the spiritual evolution of the animals concerned.

I feel that it is most clearly stated in The Bible, and also in many ancient oriental religions such as Buddhism and Hinduism to which vegetarianism dates back, that we must live in a vegetarian way; a totally compassionate way exercising that compassion to all beings, whether they are human beings or whether they are animal beings.

Scientific research suggests that we should be vegetarian for health reasons, for economical reasons and, of course, truly for compassionate reasons. I urge every one of my readers to thoroughly look into a vegetarian or vegan way of life for their own sake and for the sake of the world.

In the face of the threat of world hunger due to the population explosion, the time has now come when it is necessary to become vegetarian. A large majority of the world's population now subsists on a predominantly vegetarian diet. There is an old nutritional belief that diets containing animal protein are necessarily superior to those composed of vegetable proteins. This concept was originally based on reports showing that the physical and mental development of consumers of animal foods was generally superior to that of people on vegetarian diets. It may surprise you to know that many top ranking athletes are totally vegetarian and many are also vegan.

I would like to consider the vegetarian or vegan diet from a natural standpoint. Anatomically, man does not resemble a carnivorous creature whose short intestine is designed for rapid expulsion of decomposing flesh and contains an excess of hydrochloric acid which breaks down the harmful toxins in flesh. The hydrochloric acid present is ten times more in quantity than that found in a human being.

Carnivores have savage sharp claws and teeth or fangs designed for tearing flesh. That is how they were created. They were part of a natural cycle of balance to ensure survival of the fittest and removal of the dead, injured and diseased. They have a reason for eating meat. In its rightful place and with the proper intention, that is nature's way. Humankind eats meat for self-gratification, comfort and ease of living.

Man more closely resembles the relatively frugivorous great apes. The vegetarian animals have long bowels for digesting vegetable matter and their teeth and jaws are designed for chewing and grinding; not tearing flesh. The enzyme ptyalin is present in the saliva for the primary digestion of starches.

The fact that mankind has attempted to become carnivorous does not mean that we have been successful. I feel that our thinking now must be revised in the light of more recent research on the nutritional value of plant proteins. Many scientific studies have shown that several plant proteins can be used together so that the resulting combination can have a higher nutritional value than the individual proteins alone.

Food, it must be remembered, is intimately related to physical health and spiritual well being or its opposite. It is the bloodstream with its marvellous distribution system which carries the essential agents that provide the energy and vitality for every part of the functioning of the organism. What we eat today will be in our bloodstream within twenty four hours, or to put it another way, how we will fare, both physically and spiritually within the next twenty four hours from now, depends on the nature of the food we have taken into our stomach today.

I believe that parents should be vegetarian and should also bring up their children to favour a vegetarian or vegan diet. That way we would have a healthier population over a matter of time and I think, as a nation, we would become more compassionate and spiritual.

Meat, fish and fowl and alcoholic drinks and drugs take a heavy toll of man's health both physically and spiritually. Man, I feel, should make an earnest endeavour to lead a totally compassionate life with reverence to all God's creation. A serene and pure life is the royal road back to God.

According to the Old Testament, human beings began life by eating only fresh fruit and vegetables. The Essenes, an Israelite brotherhood living on the shores of the Dead Sea, have been in existence for approximately two hundred years before the birth of Christ. They were highly religious and did not believe in the sacrifice of animals. Since they did not believe in harming any of God's creatures, the Essenes were strictly vegetarian. Jesus, an Essene, followed the vegetarian way of life throughout his earthly existence. When he spoke of meat, he referred to food of a vegetarian nature.

The Reverend Holmes Gore tells us that the Greek word we translate as 'meat' merely means food or nourishment. Jesus Christ further said: *"If you eat living foods, the same will quicken you, but if you kill your food, the dead food will kill you also."* How can we better serve God and man than by lessening the sum total of human depravity. Meat consumption, I feel is the chief cause of crime in all its various forms and by which our own and very many other countries are cursed.

Mahatma Ghandi, a peacemaker, much beloved by his fellow countrymen, was also a vegetarian. In Ghandi's words: *"It ill becomes us to invoke in our daily prayers the blessings of God the Compassionate if we in turn will not practice elementary compassion towards our fellow creatures"*. He is also remembered for the words: *"Judge a nation on the way it treats its animals."*

We, as human beings, have to be ethical about all forms of life and to look upon life, all life, as sacred; to look upon the plants and animals as our fellow humans.

Reverence for life was taught by all the great spiritual teachers: Jesus, Krishna and Gautama the Buddha. They were all featured as good shepherds. Jesus said that we must respect the brotherhood of all life. Whoever is not kind to all forms of life, to man, to beast, to bird and all creeping things, cannot expect the blessings of the Holy One.

Gautama the Buddha became known as the Lord of Compassion for his teachings of kindness towards all living beings.

Hindu scriptures tell us that wise people see the divine breath in everything; in the elephant, in the beasts, in the cattle, in the dogs, in the birds, even in the insects. The Lord Krishna taught deep love and respect for the animal kingdom.

In recent years it was my great pleasure to personally know Linda McCartney, whom I feel did more than many others of our generation to promote vegetarianism and a deep respect for all creation. Alas, she is no longer amongst us in physical presence but I know she will continue to work for the good of God's creation from the golden realms.

Jesus said: *"In order to enter the kingdom of heaven we must become as a little child"*. The growing child naturally loves the little God-guided creatures. Children are given pets and cuddly animal toys in order to nurture that loving and protective instinct that many children feel towards an animal smaller than themselves and dependent upon them for their survival in captivity. These children often show a greater tenderness towards animals than they are able to exhibit towards human beings. They are more able to communicate this love on a telepathic wavelength with an animal than the physical difficulty of speech with their own kind.

I feel that we must look upon all animals as our spiritual brothers and sisters. We must assist them to reach a higher level of spiritual consciousness. We can only do that with love, compassion and feeling for them and by never misusing them in any way.

Sai Baba has said that in order to become spiritually liberated we must become vegetarian.

Think on these things and follow your conscience. There is so much more to life than the pleasure of the palate.

There is the whole of eternity.

A meditation for loving kindness

Sit quietly with a straight back and gently close your eyes. Feel the rhythm of the breath as it enters and leaves the body. Allow yourself to let go of the past and the here and now.

Draw your mind from your entire being, right up beyond the blue sky. Link with infinity. See all the stars, the galaxies, the sun, the moon. Travel beyond into the pure golden light realms. Hear heavenly angel voices. Feel that every part of you has become one with the entire cosmic mind, God.

You are surrounded and permeated by golden light energy. Feel this radiant energy saturating every cell and atom throughout every part of your body.

See the golden light energy all around you, filling your entire environment, suffusing the whole area in which you are living with golden light, peace, love and bliss.

See the golden light extending beyond your own immediate surroundings, travelling throughout the whole world.

View Planet Earth from space, surrounded and permeated by this lovely sense of peace and bliss and golden light energy. Feel as if you could embrace the whole of Planet Earth with your heart. Infuse love into all beings, into all creation. Feel at one with all creation. Know yourself to be in a state of utter bliss.

When you are ready, turn your mind intention back within

yourself. Feel very good, very peaceful, very calm.
   Slowly open your eyes and gently return to your world.

This very simple, healing meditation should be practised morning and evening for ten or fifteen minutes at a time. If you have a few minutes during the day, sitting peacefully and quietly, anywhere, visualise with mind intent the golden loving light from high up within the heavenly realms. Bring that loving energy down into you and around you. Bathe all of creation with the golden, loving light.

People ask the question "When is the best time of the day to meditate?" I quote an Indian Chief:

> *"In the morning when the sun is rising across the hills and the first song of the birds is heard; when the early morning dew carpets the earth and lies upon the flowers, you will know me and I shall dwell within your heart for the day.*
>   *In the evening just as the skylark sings its last note of the day; when the moon is rising and the sun shining beneath the horizon in all its magnificent splendour, this is the time to be still and I will be within your heart 'till sunrise."*

It is my sincere wish that the words written in this book will be of immense comfort for all those who have lost the way, are unsure of the future and have fear of leaving this planet. I feel that it is relevant for this particular time in history with so many conflicting opinions around today, causing so many to become utterly confused.

I hope this report conveys to the reader things that you wish to know about this Universe but don't know how to find out.

May God's love and blessings be with you into eternity.

Peter Hudson

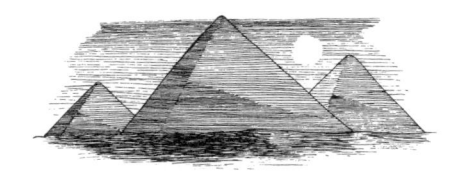

Learning through lifetimes

Did we sit, centuries ago, on marble steps beneath a canopy of vines? Vines which rambled through tall columns of pure white stone, warmed by the sun. A group of students with our mentor, captured for a fleeting moment in time as we absorbed the facts and figures imparted by the great man of learning, an orator of some skill. I can see the picture before me as if it were the work of a sculptor. The long, flowing robes reflecting the sunlight, the shades and play of light enhancing the folds and drapes of clothing. The gleam of sunlight on a pin holding a cloak in place. The absorbed look of interest and learning on the smooth faces of the students contrasting with the aged, bearded figure of the teacher.

Where are these students now? Did we travel through ancient worlds imparting these learnings to hungry minds? Did we meet and touch again in other lives, in other classrooms. Was the teacher always the same soul or did we take turns imparting our knowledge with the ebb and flow of the centuries?

Perhaps, in the shadow of the pyramid we passed on the knowledge of the ancients. Maybe even then the subject of the day was the healing properties of plants and stone. We may even have laboured within the pyramid, cutting the hieroglyphs around the Pharaoh's tomb. Did we sit beside the Nile, eating figs and drinking wine; watching the ships as they danced in the waters, learning of the wonders of the old world, marvelling at the treasures from afar being unloaded at the quayside?

Troubled Europe would have sent teacher and students underground. Books would have to be hidden, their possession a crime. Sadly, we would have watched knowledge burning. But forever in our hearts and minds, the written word is engraved. No one can touch this wealth. Unseen it can be passed on until once again learning comes without fear.

Were we perhaps burned at the stake for our interests? Caught with a basket of herbs and branded as witches. Did we gather plants from around the cottage door and venture further afield into meadow, hedgerow and forest and deep within the peaty soil? Did we learn and teach of the potions and concoctions that we steeped, boiled and ground to release their medicinal potential?

Were you hidden within monastery walls ministering to the sick and wounded, your notes inscribed with the quill by me and illuminated by my son? Slow, silent work interrupted by prayer and contemplation and the occasional frugal meal. Perhaps when I had finished writing the notes I would have worked in the gardens taking the sun into my eyes as I tended the herbs and the vegetables, maybe bringing a flower for my son to copy onto the page. No click of a button with instant results here. Long painstaking hours, eyes straining in the half-light, the work finished by the light of a candle. But how those colours will continue to glow throughout the centuries.

Victorian England would have been a difficult time. Rows of frightened children cowering from the whistling cane as the master held forth, forcing unnecessary facts into cold, hungry brains, Maybe I was the child who brought the master a frog in a jam jar or treasures collected on the long, muddy walk to school. Appeasement perhaps from a terrified child.

The present life gives us a sharing of talents. We have grown since those days on the marble steps beneath the vines. I still have the need to learn, the desire to listen but this time with unlimited possibilities for the distribution of this learning.

Who knows how many more lifetimes will incorporate this time of shared learning and teaching. Perhaps one day I can take out the file marked 'Education' from the Record of Life and all will be revealed. Lifetimes of 'Satisfactory, could do better' displayed forever before me.

Barbara Bush
Travelling with Tamarind

Heredity

Every human being is born into a generation and each generation is a link in a chain of unbroken history. Through my parents I inherit my genes, but as soon as I begin to develop, a new factor comes in which is not parents, nor my ancestry, nor past mankind, but I, my own self. And this is the important central issue. What matters most in my life is not my heredity; that only gives me my opportunity or my obstacle, my good or my bad material, but it is what I make of my heredity and not what my heredity makes of me. The past of the world, bygone humanity, my ancestors are there in me; but I myself am the artist of my life and my actions.

And then there is the present, there are my contemporaries as well as my ancestors. The life of today enters into me, offers me new material, shapes me by its influence. I am invaded, changed and partly recreated by my environment. But there again, the individual comes in. What is superbly important is what I make of this invading present and not what it makes of me.

SRI AUROBINDO FROM 'SYNTHESIS OF YOGA'

Jouissance

Sing my soul to the ocean,
sunny sea, soothe my soul,
rough waves take the pain away.
I love you, water,
aquatic nectar,
make me dance
let me howl
like a wild creature,
ride your rolling breast,
swim across the wave's crest
into the silver path of the sun,
follow the spinnakers sails of red.
Myriads of sea water droplets are shed,
cruise and soothe off my body,
tightened and rejuvenated.
Sing my soul to the ocean!

Elizabeth Jenks

Builder of hedgerows

When my time on this beautiful earth is through, it is comforting to know that I shall return to the soil to be blown by the wind and filtered by rains. I will be born again in the simple beauty of the primrose, the fragrance of the bluebell and the majesty of the rose. The fragments of my earthly existence will return many times in this form, but what will happen to my spirit?

I like to think that, eventually, after its time of rest and transformation, my spirit will find its home in some celestial woodland. It will be free to construct the heavenly hedgerows, where gentle spirits wander absorbing the tranquillity that is without time.

Following the early morning mists, I will sow the individual blades of grass, forming a restful, green backdrop against which to work. From the celestial store I would select the seeds, bringing them to life and nurturing them to maturity. In the cool of the evening I would communicate with the plants and bury their roots deep in the damp, dark earth. I will summon the rains, guide the sun and orchestrate the magic of a frosty morning. There will be delicate mists to wreath around the trees, leaving sparkling crystals on cobwebs and seeding grass. Birdsong and rustling wings enhancing the scene; insects and scurrying creatures building their homes in sandy banks and fallen trees.

Harmony of colour, scent and form would give pleasure to all who passed that way. Simple joy given by the curling of a tendril, the curve of a leaf, the unfolding of petals in the sunlight. Everywhere, the delicate, unseen fragrance held in the clear air, accompanying the rustle of leaves that shelter the woodland floor. There would be blackberries in differing shades of ripening; rose hips glowing in the sunshine; honeysuckle and clematis tangling through the branches.

I would rest in my hedgerow. With my back against the bark of an eternal tree, soft grass cushioning my weightless spiritual body, I would sit and plan tomorrow's tasks. Old growth to be cleared away and replanted with new; seeds to be caught as they fall and planted with others to form cameos of endless beauty. I would dust the leaves and polish the petals in preparation for the new day. Newly arrived souls would be welcomed to my little bit of heaven and given space and time to rest.

This could be a never-ending task throughout eternity. With the changing of the seasons, old growth and new shoots would live in peaceful harmony, each becoming the other in its time. This would be no toil, just a labour of love and deep contentment.

But even a contented spirit needs to change and grow. Eventually, I would need to seek out other lessons, different tasks for the soul, as I progressed throughout eternity. I would reluctantly bid farewell to my hedgerows, leaving a small part of me, a fleeting memory, flowering in the wild rose.

There will be other spirits to follow on and plant their own little bits of heaven. I just hope they like wild roses too.

Barbara Bush
Travelling with Tamarind

Words of wisdom, comfort and beauty

"This book is for all those who, in the noise and stress of this material world, feel the deep need of a truer meaningfulness, purpose and direction of what the true reason of their lives really is and hopefully for those of my readers who may share with me in finding a truly blissful way; perhaps the only way to the Father within."

PETER HUDSON

"You are wherever your thoughts are. Make sure your thoughts are where you want to be. For the true believer, believing is seeing. Better to be a fool who believes everything than a sceptic who believes nothing - not even the truth."

LIVING TAO 42

"Nature is great because it is simple."

LAO TZU

"There is also the aspect that man has a responsibility, a great responsibility, towards what is regarded as a lower form of creation, because animals and humans are part of life equally with the tree, the fruit, the flower, the vegetable, the bird. All life moves forward together, or backward together. Thus, if man displays the divine qualities of love, mercy and compassion, then the wolf can lie down with the lamb."

SILVER BIRCH

To the Citizens of the World

How long
Can you abuse a friend?
How long
Before you lose a friend?
How long
Can your money making last
Before you realise
The Golden Age has passed?
The things you think you own
Are only yours on loan -
Today you throw a loaded dice
Will you be around to pay the price?

THOMAS RYEMARSH

"I have emphasised the wonderful power of the spirit within you. I have told of the charts of your lives, which will be shown to you when you pass over and the responsibility for your actions and thoughts which lies with each of you.

Meditation has been shown to be all important in your lives and the need of control of thought which can be attained by constant practice.

I gave you glimpses of the spheres. This knowledge will enable you to picture your loved ones whom you will never again think of as being 'lost'.

I have explained that thought is a substance and described how we use it as a force here in the World of Light.

I have shown you the purpose of your lives on earth and described the right attitude for you to take of the change you call death.

I have shown that everything in life and in the universes is a question of vibration and in this connection that the ideas of a future life in some far off place is false; you have to dispense with your definitions of time and space.

I have pointed out that science is now nearing the position in which the psychic sense will be closely studied and belief in the etheric body will be established."

Summary from Fragments of Truth from the Unseen
by Dr Hamilton as given to Beatrice Russell.

"There are billows far out on the ocean that never break on the beach. There are thoughts in the temple of silence too great for our hearts to speak."

PARAMAHANSA YOGANANDA

"God holds the key to all unknown and I am glad: if someone else should hold the key - or if he trusted it to me, I might be sad."

UNKNOWN

"Every moment as it passes is of infinite value for it is the representative of a whole eternity."

GOETHE

"Prayer is not asking. It is a longing of the soul."

GHANDI

"Actually, death is something very friendly. We can salute it as we would a birth. Because it is always the same process, whether we come or go, it's just crossing to another dimension. Because the human being who is dying is going to another dimension, we could learn to welcome the death. His learning on earth passes and he prepares for another level, eventually to be-come again. We who stay here will miss him and suffer the loss. It's only a short while that we are separated; our hour will also come and our desire will be fulfilled.."

Dr Dagmar Berg

The Way

"The early Christians called themselves Seekers. They did not say they were Seekers for the Heaven, but they said they were Seekers for The Way. It was always The Way. In the Akashic Records you constantly find those words - The Way.

You see, there was not a church, there was no dogma or creed, no ceremonial at all; just The Way and the Way was The Way of Life and The Way of Life was the Way of Unconditional Love. That is what we are trying to teach."

Dr Lascelles from Spirit

For the unified mind in accord with the way,
all self-centred striving ceases.
Doubts and irresolutions vanish
and life in true faith is possible.
With a single stroke we are freed from bondage;
nothing clings to us and we hold to nothing.
All is empty, clear, self-illuminating,
with no exertion of the mind's power.
Here thought, feeling, knowledge and imagination
are of no value.
In this world of suchness there is neither self nor
other-than-self.
To come directly into harmony with this reality
just simply say when doubts arise,
"not two".
In this "not two" nothing is separate,
nothing is excluded.
No matter when or where,
enlightenment means entering this truth.
And this truth is beyond extension
or diminution in time or space;
in it a single thought
is ten thousand years.

HSING HSING MING
SENGSTAN THIRD ZEN PATRIARCH
ENGLISH TRANSLATION - RICHARD B CLARKE

Prayer

Oh Lord, we ask Thee to open up Thy Heaven still wider that the prayers of these people may penetrate still further into Thy Heaven, and that the angels that minister unto these that pray may come nearer every day.
    The jewel that these people have set in this country of England does not yet shine in the fullness of its brilliance. Lord, make it shine so that it may be seen by all people of the world.
    Give unto its light the power to give comfort to those that are weary, health to those that are sick and the Kingdom of Heaven to those that pray. Amen

UNKNOWN

Jesus said: "You shall love the Lord your God with all your heart and with all your soul and with all your mind. This is the greatest and first commitment."

(MATTHEW 22:37-38)

"Love is the golden ladder upon which the heart mounts to heaven."

AMERICAN LYCEUM MANUAL

"The best service any book can render is to impart truth to make you think it out for yourself."

ELBERT HUBBARD

"It is only in the depth of silence that the voice of God can be heard."

SAI BABA

> Earth awakens from its winter
> the pit of its belly makes peace with the storms and rain,
> a gentle breath softens the pain
>
> But listen!
> In the quiet, someone crying still remains,
> I watch the rising-falling breath
> until the sobs slow down and come to rest
>
> and now! Shadows fade with the final tear
> the buds exhilarate with coming change
> and birds resound their heart songs in the trees
>
> Come! Open an eye and see so clear
> life once more so rich, so strange.
> I drink full, deep, of its mysteries.

OS, LIVING TAO

"We must learn to respect and love our Earth just as the ancients did. The ancient Greeks looked upon Earth as our Mother, a living being. They called her Gaia, the goddess who gives all God's creatures, including ourselves, sustenance.

Oh, Gaia, Mother divine, we bless you. You feed all life in our world, whether it be plant, tree, insect, bird, animal or ourselves. You give us nourishment from your very soul and we in return give you thanks and love."

"Chi produces the human body just as water becomes ice. As water freezes into ice, so Chi coagulates to form the human body. When ice melts, it becomes water. When a person dies, he or she becomes spirit again. It is called spirit, just as melted ice changes its name to water."

WANG CHONG AD 27-97

"Think what a mystery life is. It emerges from the unknown and into the unknown it dissolves. We have learned much but we are still picking up pebbles on the vast seashore of the spirit."

PARAMAHANSA YOGANANDA

"This day you will be with me in Paradise."

LORD JESUS CHRIST

Time Running Out

Lord, you made a perfect Heaven on Earth
For all of us
And some of us believed it,
But haven't we done well -
We've made a perfect Hell on Earth
And now we're beginning to believe it.

THOMAS RYEMARSH

"Spiritual hunger is the ultimate meaning of every activity in life. The dissatisfaction and the restlessness that remain even after obtaining all the necessities of life show that everyone consciously or unconsciously does suffer from spiritual hunger and it is not appeased until the spirit within is realised. Without this divine discontent there is no real progress."

SAI BABA

Deep peace of the quiet earth to you.
Deep peace of the shining stars to you.
Deep peace of the Son of Peace to you.

"Don't worry about middle age - you'll soon grow out of it."

UNKNOWN

Lest we forget

Animals and humans
Of equal worth
Saved by the Ark
To inherit the Earth,
With love and respect for each other,
As sister and brother;
Ask anyone who knows -
The tail that wags
And, in the eyes, it shows -

Man who sees himself as 'Boss'
His animals entered under -
'Profit and Loss' -

If only the tables would turn
To make him wiser -
To make him learn.

THOMAS RYEMARSH

"The truth will make you free."

THOMAS A'KEMPIS

"When your work is done, then withdraw! That is the Way of Heaven."

TAOISM

Contentment

What does the townsman know of life?
I pity him.
He cannot hear the songbirds sing
Their morning hymn.
The sun arising o'er the hills
To gild the skies
A glory sheds that is not seen
By townsmen's eyes.
The miracle of each new spring
That life unfolds,
And country lanes fresh-clad in green
He ne'er beholds.
As swelling buds unfurl their leaves,
And blossoms flower,
With thankful mind
I live and drink
Each peaceful hour.
Oh! Not for me the city rush,
The crowded train,
The jostling, noisy, tinsel world,
The fevered brain.
Content am I my days to spend
In quiet retreat,
Unknown, unpraised, but praising God
As think I meet.

ROSEMARY BROWN

"We are too anxious about the things in time and ignore the eternity within us."

Thomas A'Kempis

Leisure

What is this life if, full of care,
We have no time to stand and stare.

No time to stand beneath the boughs
And stare as long as sheep or cows.

No time to see, when woods we pass,
Where squirrels hide their nuts in grass.

No time to see, in broad daylight,
Streams full of stars like skies at night.

No time to turn at Beauty's glance,
And watch her feet, how they can dance.

No time to wait till her mouth can
Enrich that smile her eyes began.

A poor life this if, full of care,
We have no time to stand and stare.

W H Davies

Be at Peace

"You are Spirit - not a physical body or organic nervous system. Although temporarily in a physical body you are unaffected by it.

Being Spirit, nothing can ever harm or hurt you. You are Spirit; perfectly calm and peaceful. You easily push away all mental and physical burdens thus allowing pure love, through God, to manifest and permeate every atom and cell of your being.

You are peaceful and in a wonderful world of bliss at all times because you and God are One."

PETER HUDSON

"Try to realise you are a divine traveller. You are here for only a little while then depart for a dissimilar and fascinating world. Do not limit your life to one small life and one small earth. Remember the vastness of the spirit that dwells within you. Let God flow through you continuously."

PARAMAHANSA YOGANANDA

The Lord God said: 'It is not good that man should be alone; I will make him a helper fit for him". So the Lord God formed every beast of the field and every bird of the air, and brought them to man.

GENESIS 2: 18-19.

"Commune with your own heart in meditation and it will tell you that this life on Earth is not the end. God has allowed part of the veil to be lifted so that man need no longer be left in doubt. Many more people than you have dreamed of have been able to look beyond the veil and know the truth, helped by those on the other side."

Dr Hamilton as given to Beatrice Russell

In a City

Amid the city traffic's droning din. By noise besieged, where fumes the nose assail. Recoiling from it all, my senses reel, I wonder what the turmoil can avail.
There's scarcely space for God himself to breathe, and by such noise His voice is surely drowned. It seems He's being crowded out of life, the whole machines the modern world confound. Oh, stop the wheels and stop the hustling cars; the endless crocodile that onward winds. For if we lose the way to quietude, we'll surely lose our hearing and our minds.

Rosemary Brown

"When one of you on the earth plane strives to help another, a thousand in the higher realms are urging you on."

Silver Birch

"The key to the development of the spiritual faculties lies in everyone seeking to live and to manifest their will in harmony with the immutable laws of nature and ethereal divine energies which are created through mind energy fields, thus uniting with the entire universal force, God, and becoming one with God."

PETER HUDSON

"Any time you become fascinated by some material creation, just close your eyes and look within and contemplate its source. Even if all matter were to melt into nothingness there could be not one iota of vacant space. Space empty of spirit, forms of creation in the great void; both are equally pervaded by spirit."

PARAMAHANSA YOGANANDA

"We shall know the Truth and the Truth shall make us free."

JESUS CHRIST

"Chi manifests itself in this world as a sort of radiation that is invisible to the ordinary eye but can be clearly seen by advanced adepts who have cultivated this ability. Chi can also be detected and measured by sophisticated technology."

DR E HOWELL (50 YEARS RESEARCHING SUBTLE ENERGIES)

"Cultivate the feeling of expansion. Your soul nature is of the present. Your home is eternity."

Paramahansa Yogananda

"I sing the body electric."

Walt Whitman

> In this body, in this town of the Spirit
> There is a little house shaped
> like a lotus, and in that house
> there is a little space. One should
> know what is there.
>
> What is there? Why is it so important?
>
> There is as much in that space
> within the heart, as there is
> in the whole world outside.
>
> Heaven, earth, fire, wind, sun,
> moon, lightning, stars; whatever
> is and whatever is not, everything is there.

Chandyoga Upanishad

"To the four quarters of the world I send compassion. To the north, south, east and west, above and below, I send compassion."

Unknown

"When you endeavour to experience your spiritual convictions, another world begins to open up to you."

Paramahansa Yogananda

"When I look at the sky which you have made, at the moon and stars which you set in their places - what is man, that you think of him; mere man, that you care for him?"

Psalm 8.3-4

Taoist Meditation

> Close your eyes and you will see clearly.
> Cease to listen and you will hear Truth.
> Be silent and your heart will sing.
> Seek no contacts and you will find union.
> Be still and you will move forward on the tide of the Spirit.
> Be gentle and you will need no strength.
> Be patient and you will achieve all things.
> Be humble and you will remain entire.

"Help as much as you can, as silently as you can, as lovingly as you can; leave the rest to God, who gave you the chance to serve."

Sai Baba

"Be still and empty for God shall fill your heart and soul with far greater love than you could ever wish for. So much further beyond all words and thoughts is He. I know no other means than not to speak than being empty and still."

UNKNOWN

A Contemplation

Inner peace, inner calm
Rest assured,
My mind, my friend
Elect to meditate
In pure ecstatic state,
Leave the turmoil of the day,
The strife, the pain,
Slip into unconsciousness
Supreme and Blue,
Tender and true.

All the colours of the mind
Rise within the soul,
Creating an ambience
Of mind, balanced and calm,
Serene life enhancing seva
You have enriched my inner self
And enabled contemplation
Forever.

ELIZABETH JENKS

"We should train ourselves to think eternity; infinity; God is everywhere; God is love."

Paramahansa Yogananda

"Be like flowers which send their fragrance without speaking of their own excellence. Imitate the sun who shines likewise."

> From the unreal lead me to the real.
> From darkness lead me to the light.
> From death lead me to immortality.

Buddha

"In contemplation of created things, by steps we may ascend to God."

American Lyceum Manual

"The soul is not more than the body and the body is not more than the soul and there is no object so soft but it makes a hub for the wheel'd universe."

Walt Whitman 'Song of Myself'

"I and my Father are ONE."

Jesus Christ

Celtic Blessing

May the road rise with you
May the wind be always at your back
May the sun shine warm upon your face
May the rain fall soft upon your fields
Until we meet again...
May God hold you in the hollow of his hand.

The Author

Peter Hudson has spent forty years in the practice and study of natural medicine including Ayurvedic and Traditional Chinese medicine.

He holds professional qualifications in naturopathy, osteopathy, herbal medicine, homoeopathy and clinical nutrition. He has run highly successful clinics in Knightsbridge, London, Kent and Sussex.

Currently he specialises in holistic and preventive health care as a means to achieving and maintaining health and wellbeing.

He also lectures and conducts seminars and courses on holistic medicine and is the author of published books and research papers.

Index

Animals 42-46, 47-53
Atom 9-12, 19, 37

Bible 13
Bio-magnetism 39
Bio-plasmic 17
Biological 16
Birth 9
Black Hole 12, 38
Body 9, 11
Building blocks 14
Buried 17

Carnivorous 49
Chemicals 13
Chi energy 22
Chi Kung 40
Chinese medicine 28
Christ 9
Consciousness 13, 20
Cosmic mind 20
Creativity 8
Cremation 17

Death 9-17
Decomposition 14, 16
Destruction 9
Dimension 10, 12
Disease 28

Earth 12, 18
Earthly body 10

Einstein 9
Electricity 23
Electro-dynamic 15
Electro-magnetic 16, 18, 21
Electro-static 18
Electromagnetism 8, 9
Electrons 11, 14
Element 14
Emotional body 32
Energy 8, 9, 11
Energy body 12
Enlightening 11
Essenes 51
Eternity 10
Evidence 11

Father 9
Fields 19
Food 14
Force 9, 14
Free will 9

Galaxy 12
God 8, 23, 31, 39
Golden light 41
Gravity 19

Heaven 22
Human 8

Illness 28
Immortal 27

Intelligence 10
Investigation 10
Invisible 12
Iso-electric 19

Jesus Christ 9, 39

Karma 43
Kirlian photography 28

Laws 10, 18
Life 9-10
Life force 14, 18, 27
Light 9
Light energy body 12
Love 9, 13, 24

Magnetic fields 40
Malnutrition 35
Mantra 21
Mass 9
Material 9
Materialism 24
Matter 9
McCartney, Linda 52
Meat 14, 49-53
Meditation 11, 20, 21
Medium 11
Mercury 33
Metabolic rate 20
Milky Way 12
Mind 11, 20, 26, 30
Mind field 27
Mineral kingdom 33
Modern science 15
Molecular elements 15
Molecules 14
Mystic 11

Nature 12, 16

Near death experience 25, 31
Neutrons 11, 14
Nuclear bomb 23
Nucleus 18

Orthodox 11, 13
Out-of-body experience 31

Particles 9, 14, 37
Personality 8, 9, 14
Philosopher 15
Physical 10, 11
Physicists 12, 14
Physics 12
Physiological 16
Physiologist 15
Plane 11
Plants 16
Proof 11
Protein 14
   Plant 50
Protons 11, 14
Psychological problems 20
Pythagoras 33

Quantum physics 8

Radio waves 23
Reality 12
Realms 10
Regeneration 9
Reincarnation 9, 42
Religion 8
Research 10
Russian research 16

School 13
Science
   Breakthroughs 11
   Investigations 8

VIDEO INFORMATION

Tai Chi Chi Kung

THE ART OF CULTIVATING THE UNIVERSAL HEALING FORCE

by Peter Hudson

Professionally filmed video illustrating this gentle self-healing art form for optimum health and happiness. Demonstrated and written by Peter Hudson, Holistic and Natural Medicine Practitioner, Teacher and Author with over 40 years of experience in the Natural Healing Arts.

The location for the video is on the high cliffs of Sussex overlooking the sea, beautifully set against clear blue skies and the freshness of grass and trees. A perfect setting.

Recorded specially for this video is a unique musical composition which inspires, relaxes and creates a state of inner balance, calm and bliss.

Daily practice for as little as 15 minutes, instructed and accompanied by the video, creates a protective shield that assists the body to handle the stresses of present day living.

A useful informative guide to the successful practice of Tai Chi Chi Kung is included.

The UK price for the video is £14.99 plus £2.00 postage and packing

Available from Mayfair Publishing, PO Box 860, Eastbourne, East Sussex BN20 7DJ, United Kingdom

Scientific
   Evidence 11
   Investigations 8
Self-realisation 18
Senses 12
Sensory experiences 37
Solar energy 23
Solar-system 12
Soul 9, 27
   Evolution 42
Speed of light 9
Spine 16
Spirit 9
Spiritual 9, 10
Spiritual body 17
Spiritual dimension 13
Spiritual experience 11
Spiritual world 13
Sub-atomic particles 23
Sun 12
Survival 8, 11

Tai Chi Chi Kung 28
Tao 29
Thought field 27
Transition 10, 12

Universal mind 21
Universe 9, 11, 12, 23

Vegan 48
Vegetarian 45-46, 47-51
Vibration 8, 12, 17-18, 33
Visible light spectrum 19
Visionary 11

World 8

Yin and Yang 22

Zen 17

BOOK INFORMATION

Travelling with Tamarind

by Barbara Bush

A bedside book of gentle healing meditations and cameos inspired by the world of nature.

A well loved farm in Devon; hours spent sitting among the cliffs of the Cornish coast watching the waves from magnificent collision to gentle calm; days of sunshine and shadow in the English Lake District; a healing moor in Austria; walks over the Yorkshire Moors; these are a selection of the inspirations that lay behind this gentle book.

Travelling with Tamarind is the first book produced by Barbara Bush. The stories were originally written for her own pleasure, often inspired by, and written for, friends and family and given as gifts. With the reactions to these gifts it soon became obvious that there was a need in the world for a gentle book based on simple meditations and observations of the countryside. What could be more calming and peaceful than a walk through the woods and meadows of your mind with a companion.

ISBN 1 898572 04 6

Travelling with Tamarind is priced at £6.99 per copy plus 50p postage and packing, from Tamarind, Mayfair Publishing PO Box 860, Eastbourne East Sussex BN20 7DJ

The book would make an ideal gift for a special friend or people unable, through age or infirmity, to walk down country lanes and look at the stars.